HEALED

All rights reserved

Published by:
Global Vision Publishing
Fort Lauderdale, FL

Copyright @ 2022 Jaroslav Vasicko

All rights reserved. No part of this book may be reproduced by any means, nor transmitted, nor stored in a retrieval system, nor translated into a machine language, in any form or by any means, electronic, mechanical, photocopying, recording, or otherwise, without the prior written permission of the author.

Jaroslav Vasicko – www.JaroslavVasicko.com

Global Vision Publishing – www.GlobalVisionPublishing.com

Edited by: Sterling Jr.
Cover and Back Cover painted by: Tyler Murphy
Design and Video Recording by: Jobin Daniel and Michelle Aley Abi

Printed in the United States of America

ISBN: 979-8-9857948-1-6

One man's journey of awakening, healing and transformation in poems

Inspired by real events and the Holy Spirit

Painted by Tyler Murphy

Edited by Sterling Jr

*Design & Video Recording
Jobin Daniel and Michelle Aley Abi*

Testimonials

> I have the privilege to know Jari, and so grateful for him and his life. Just amazed at the call of God on Jari's life and how the Lord is walking with him in a very special way. To see this book being published is a testimony of the faithfulness of God in and through Jari. Every poem is profound with a deep sense of gratitude to the Lord and from a place of assurance that "all things work together for good for those who love Him and are called according to His purpose", in spite the deep scars that Jari bears only to know that it's God's love that rescues and which he in return can offer.
>
> -Pastor Jimmy Thomas

> A great compilation of heart felt expressions of a man's spiritual journey into God's Love! If you want to feel shaken and inspired to look deeper into how God's mysterious Ways are working in your life, I highly recommend Jari's book!
>
> -Dr Jelena Petkovic

> How can we question the purpose of brokenness when we see the very thing become a work of art in the Master's hand? This book of verses by Jari Vasicko have demonstrated in profound ways how seemingly simple words can express such well-formed beauty in the crucible we call life.
>
> -Joshua K Prasad

> Wow, just wow- congratulations! So compelling and authentic, if words could dance- these would be tap dancing off the pages. Thanks so much for sharing, you are an inspiration!
>
> -David Black

> Raw and riveting! Words woven by a poet setting hearts on fire, one page at a time...
>
> -Karina Belkin

> This book of poetry entries is a beautifully correlated and woven together, allowing nonconformist and conformist people to look in the window of Mr. Vasickos's world in a sensitive time and see his present transformation and work for the greater good all for the glory of God.
>
> -Wanda Allen

> Like David of old, Jari before God lays bare his soul. With naked honesty, he holds nothing back to be forever free. Breathing in, breathing out, rising and falling yet to rise again, he takes us through the paces of his journey allowing us to join him. I loved how it ends with "FORTY," as to bring finality to the endless wanderings of our prodigal minds, back home safe at last with the Father.
>
> -Ken Purvis,
> The Glorious Restoration

To all the misfits everywhere,

Find your voice and God, and follow them. They are waiting to be discovered. I am one of you. I love you. I walk with you and Him on this journey of happy destiny and salvation. It is the greatest gift of all. May this book inspire you in your struggle and serve as a living amens to those I hurt in mine.

Your friend always,
Jari

Testimonials

> I have the privilege to know Jari, and so grateful for him and his life. Just amazed at the call of God on Jari's life and how the Lord is walking with him in a very special way. To see this book being published is a testimony of the faithfulness of God in and through Jari. Every poem is profound with a deep sense of gratitude to the Lord and from a place of assurance that "all things work together for good for those who love Him and are called according to His purpose", in spite the deep scars that Jari bears only to know that it's God's love that rescues and which he in return can offer.
>
> -Pastor Jimmy Thomas

> A great compilation of heart felt expressions of a man's spiritual journey into God's Love! If you want to feel shaken and inspired to look deeper into how God's mysterious Ways are working in your life, I highly recommend Jari's book!
>
> -Dr Jelena Petkovic

> How can we question the purpose of brokenness when we see the very thing become a work of art in the Master's hand? This book of verses by Jari Vasicko have demonstrated in profound ways how seemingly simple words can express such well-formed beauty in the crucible we call life.
>
> -Joshua K Prasad

> Wow, just wow- congratulations! So compelling and authentic, if words could dance- these would be tap dancing off the pages. Thanks so much for sharing, you are an inspiration!
>
> -David Black

> Raw and riveting! Words woven by a poet setting hearts on fire, one page at a time...
>
> -Karina Belkin

> This book of poetry entries is a beautifully correlated and woven together, allowing nonconformist and conformist people to look in the window of Mr. Vasickos's world in a sensitive time and see his present transformation and work for the greater good all for the glory of God.
>
> -Wanda Allen

> Like David of old, Jari before God lays bare his soul. With naked honesty, he holds nothing back to be forever free. Breathing in, breathing out, rising and falling yet to rise again, he takes us through the paces of his journey allowing us to join him. I loved how it ends with "FORTY," as to bring finality to the endless wanderings of our prodigal minds, back home safe at last with the Father.
>
> -Ken Purvis,
> The Glorious Restoration

To all the misfits everywhere,

Find your voice and God, and follow them. They are waiting to be discovered. I am one of you. I love you. I walk with you and Him on this journey of happy destiny and salvation. It is the greatest gift of all. May this book inspire you in your struggle and serve as a living amens to those I hurt in mine.

Your friend always,

Jari

1 Arresting Fears (Endless Love)

Put all my fears, in arrears,
dear Father of mine,
remove old blocks, reset clocks,
please show me you're kind.

Make all my fears, disappear,
before I choke or drown,
you promise rest, so let me dwell,
In Your presence lie down.

Please break these chains,
lift this curse, on my knees I beg You,
tired, torn, how much more,
can this body endure?

Having fought a bloody fight
with the enemy,
with the thief that comes only by night,
to steal, destroy and kill.

My soul it wants - and take my peace -
he has already done so,
Your mercy, grace, is all that's left,
Your divine light and glow.

Or myself, did I wrestle with,
in the muddy pits?
Digging deep to find, try let go,
that which no longer fits.

And is it love that I am looking for
and have been this whole time?
You say yes, a good guess,
O' sweet child of mine.

Arrest my fears and the evil one,
imagined or real,
cover me with endless love,
its warmth let me feel.

2 Sweet Surrender (Amazing Grace)

Broken and beyond help in whispers I hear,
In the end, by myself, no one comes near.
Only the dealer man picks up my sofa,
Perfect fit for his house or daughters at Nova.

Outside the hospital, trash bag in hand,
Having pissed, shit myself, isn't this grand?
Standing in pouring rain, two Angels come, take me home, get some rest, long time had none.

Drunk again the next day, the end nowhere near, blackouts, jail, crashing cars in front and in rear. Walking the railroad tracks to end it all here or the highway, with frozen bank accounts and no hope, I did it my way!

A moment of clarity suddenly appears, all is not yet lost, a meeting is near! Walking in soaked and wet, raising my hand,
"I need help!" are the words that I said.

Must admit I am powerless - a complete defeat-such is the paradox to find Power they repeat and repeat. On the wall triangles, slogans and steps, Understand nothing yet, Hungry, distressed.

Absence of strategy, without a plan,
Just follow these simple steps remarks the man. I am facing homelessness, can you relate? You must change everything, he reiterates.

Worn out shoes, backpack on walking to meetings, bus rides, coffee pots, extending greetings. How will I make it through, bum me a cigarette, friends with the homeless man teaching me etiquette.

Humble yourself even more, here you can sleep, willing to clean the yard for little to eat. Where is God in all of this, just on the wall? You will find this Power when finished all.

All these steps he must have meant as we part ways, hurry up, get to work, no more delays!
This is just life and death, the choice is yours, blank look I give him back, sweating through all pours.

They call it surrender, a gift from above,
I call it Amazing Grace, unconditional Love.
Freed at the gates of hell, the obsession lifted, with new life and wings I have been gifted.

Thank God for everything, taught me a friend, I do on my knees each night and will 'til the end. To be first you must be last the Scriptures say, Amen to that, I say, this is the way!

3 Love Yourself

From self-loathing to "Love Yourself",
What a tall order!
Not a clue on what to do,
Total disorder.

Never taught while in school
how to practice self-care,
Not part of the curriculum
Being raised over there.

March in line, conform to this,
Be more like him, is how they rhyme.
On being self and loving it,
Nothing to say, we don't do it.

And on how to love, live and why,
totally blank, it may be so,
as if though,
Our system last ranked.

Or I missed the days they were
teaching it, totally scattered,
oops, oh well, what can I do,
now it doesn't matter.

And now that I come to think of it,
Having pondered, considered it,
It's neither here nor over there,
no courses offered on self-care.

In fact if you go anywhere In this whole crazy world, not even one single class teaches this pearl. To Love Oneself, you must be nuts, What language are you speaking? Unheard of, in all these parts, just keep on dreaming!

So I had to go down to the pits looking for answers, on how to give love to self and why it all matters. When I then re-emerged after deep digging, in shadow-side neighborhood of my inner being, I came up for air exhausted and torn, having properly examined the source of my scorn.

False belief system and improper programming, turned out to be the root cause of all of my suffering. Captive in prison cell inside of my mind, was I held without bail this entire time.

Somehow believing I am less than, not good enough, unworthy of love, became the parasites, viruses, below and above. Self will run riot as called in the rooms, self-sabotage at every step, totally doomed. This disease that wants me dead had to be outed
if I were to thrive one day, unclogged and unclouded

So replacing this damaged and defective software became the next step on my way to self-care. The Word of God, advisors, angels and Sages, purged by plant medicine, its healing for ages.

Climbing the twelve steps on my journey home, family, support system, no longer alone. Tapped into Power by which to live - higher than mine, hidden inside of me was this whole time. With it I love myself, or at least I try, no longer a prisoner of the dark side.

Having dug so so deep to plant a new root, towards the stars upwards I shoot. With brand new wiring, light on, learnt lessons, aiming straight for the sky into the heavens. Towards the light with all I've got and so much more, carrying winds of change, a lion's roar!

Learning to love myself one day at a time, one action, one gift to me if only a dime. Thank you Lord for this sweet call to transform and heal, grateful beyond measure for the Love that I feel.

# Hungry Soul

Clumsy and colossal,
in confusion it dwells,
my soul, o' my Father,
please show me the way.

sinful or divine is nature of mine?
just fog and mystery currently abide.
So many voices inside of my head,
whom to believe and whom to neglect?

Spiritual warfare in heavenly places
Inside of mind, it echoes and races,
The blood of Jesus cleanses and cleans,
being sufficient for all of my sins?

Can the devil be saved too, from the bottomless pit?
Or condemned forever in prison he sits?
The Hindu, the Buddhaa, Muhammad and Tao,
can all of them too be right somehow?

I wake in angst and desire to hear,
from you my Father as I incline you my ear.
Why did you make me, and who is my Mother,
if you are my daddy and you make life together?

Worship and praise, pure expressions of love,
or is my heart deceitful as some prophets write? Awake and raw, fearful and lost,
finding trust elusive and just beyond grasp.

Take me O' Lord, and all of me too,
remake me more neatly and squarely anew.
At midnight I cry out on a telephone line,
with others praying bonded in time.

Just one word, dear Father, please put in my soul, so I know only the Truth that cannot be fooled. Afraid more to live than to die?
How hungry for You is the soul of mine.

5 Selfless

Long to be selfless,
a surrendered soul,
with ego deflated,
selfishness gone.

Out with self-centered fear,
the root of my woes,
there's no more room
for its wrecking blows.

To my knees it took me
while in full bloom,
having manifested
destruction, doom.

Me being selfish?
Don't you know who I am?
Question my motives,
how do you dare?

Underneath that fright,
desire to be loved
and connected
do always reside.

Safe and protected,
I long to be,
finally fulfilling
this unmet need.
For how to partner,
and truly fit,
with me, other humans,
totally unfit.

Show me the way God,
I have gone astray,
mistaking directions,
in confusion, dismay.

Help me declutter
my messy shed,
remove its spoiled parts,
and layers shed.

To be free of bondage,
grant me the grace,
Humbly I ask You,
to find my place.

Please let me breathe now,
easy and slow,
without resentment,
with unclogged pores.

And that which blocked me,
creating this mess,
let me surrender,
To You, selflessness.

6 Needles (Prison Break)

Traded shared happiness
For isolation, loneliness
Stuck a needle in my arm,
Filled its veins with emptiness.

In a haystack lying there
Was the prickly pear
Reaping with it what I sowed
empty glass, blank stare.

Dr Jekyll - Mr Hyde
In fine company,
Pines and needles everywhere
Tubs of gin rummy.

Smile back with those purple teeth,
bad breath fog the mirror
A rip of filth will do the trick
Must disappear to see clearer.

Through the joints and cigarettes
Cloudy fog of perfect vision
I can see now through and thru,
Revealing fool-proof prison.

Another bite of rat poison
Capsuled chunks of dope
Flush me down the toilet
Draining out all hope.

Must I die to break from here,
The lone form of escape?
Father please deliver me
I cry out to You, I pray.

7. Higher Power

The power of We,
Not he, she, heshe,
It's us joint together
'Tis Humanity.

The power of Us,
Neither my, mine nor me,
It's Brothers and Sisters,
Leaning on WE.

So lean in my Brother
and let it all go,
In sweet surrender
Death to ego.

Arms stretched together
For we are all one
We'll catch you dear Sister
Old fears now gone.

With it old patterns,
Outdated thoughts
Burnt up in ashes
Who would have thought?

It's transformation
The growing of wings,
One tribe, one nation,
Passing old things.

To the Holy of Holies,
To the Most High
We're singing praises
For He heard well our cry.

Here for each other
Good work my love
Rest now in Power
Of WE, US as ONE.

8 Cleansing Lenses (Compassionate Heart)

With eyes of compassion
I can finally see
That which was hidden
In plain sight appears.

And with them to feel
The collective pain
In twenty twenty
To die is to gain.

The chills and the sweats,
Screaming birth pains
Undressing regrets
Unraveling chains.

The wheel is in motion
Head piercing through shell
Our transformation
We live it to tell.

In holes of wellness,
All here to get well
Purging and cleansing
Climbing from hell.

And who am I really?
Which way is up?
Am I touching the ceiling,
With dirt covered up?

Questions in knots
Untying tongued ties
Reshuffling slots
Revealing surprise.

Look through the lens
Of unconditional love
Sight filters cleansed
Compassionate heart.

And so it is so
My bruised battered friend
Blessings of healing
From the heavenly realm.

Such is the grace
Of the Creator of ours
To whom seek it is given
Overflow grand prize.

9 Taken

My heart is taken,
Not forsaken,
Is what she said.
Between the lines
I then so read:
In love with someone else.

I wonder though
Where his heart lies,
If not next to her?
How far and off
It now beats
And why not together.

How beautiful
It is to share
So authentically.
To lay it all
On the line
To express truth clearly.

And to find love,
O' what a grind
And yet to some so easy.
Others are, all alone
Worlds apart,
Making stomachs queasy.

God knows best,
kneel down, rest
Trust His divine timing,
Her words flow,
in divine glow,
reassuring me.

My heart is taken,
Not mistaken,
Into depths of faith,
Into ocean's love,
On wings of dove,
Straight to Father's arms.

10 Awakening
(From Darkness to Light)

Illusive illusion
Nail biter cut thin
Slowed to slow motion,
Let it begin.

Inverted solution
Light coming back in,
Unstuck from confusion
Where has it been?

Wake me already
From bad acid trip
Gentle, slow, steady
Barbwire, don't trip.

Allowing this riddle
To fully unfold,
Rotting core's middle
Infected with mold.

Dissent into darkness
Years of pure deceit,
Power punch harness
Defeat seems complete.

Coming to surface
Strange hold of old,
Seeking light's furnace
To be transmuted to gold.

Yearning for freedom
Its last crushing blow,
Must bow the darkness
Becoming white snow.

Transfigure mountain
By order shall move,
With authority and power
No more to prove.

Who's the guilty party
In charge of foul play,
Who committed murder
Who had the Lamb slain?

From shadowy cloudy
And hidden within,
To loud and rowdy
Displaying its sin.

Unveiling of veil pains
To tear the wall down,
Breaking off all chains
To put on His crown.

Christ revealed as Savior,
Down insidious snake
In full glory, favor,
New humanity awake.

11 Ark

Build me an ark
For the storms of life,
Flooded and drenched
I'm cut by knife.

Bloody and sore
From the wrestling match
Pour down God, pour,
I'm thirsty, quench.

Hunched over and over
Stuck in a bunch,
Are you speaking to me?
I've got a hunch.

This helter skelter
Has got to stop,
I'm seeking shelter
A resting stop.

Some may have called it
A cry for help,
For long long for refuge
For Your presence felt.

Build of me a new life
That I could live,
Harness of blindness
Release, forgive.

Each callused hardness
Reequip,
Swallow me whole
Brick by brick.

Fill in the hollow
With ease and grace,
Love on my soul
And replace.

Wash me aclean Lord,
In stunning glow,
With Your living water,
Overflow.

Bring me a wife too,
With whom to build,
For Your sake, glory
In bonded guild.

12 Take Off (Time)

Pruning and cutting,
Of the underbrush,
Was slow and steady,
And with no rush.

Go on forgetting
All those lies,
Time to get ready
For the big surprise.

Time to get ready
To open the grand prize,
To unlock the box
And open eyes.

Time to jump through
The wall at stake,
Unblock, release
Command to take.

On runway in plane
With hour at hand,
Fly now My son
Just as just you can.

Time to let go
Of the parking brake,
Time to break free
For My own sake.

And for yours too
And your family
Produce for two,
Live happily.

Time to spread wings
Soar with the rest,
Let go of all fear
I'll grant you rest.

Time to arrest
And put away for good,
All of your past,
Brand new look.

Time has arrived
For the seed to sprout,
To provide fruit
To walk with no doubt.

Greatness at hand
For My delight
Provisioned, planned
Before there was light.

It's time to show
Who I really am
Stand up, be bold,
It's the the great I AM.

13 Worthy

What am I worth,
Is it less or more?
Haven't you heard
On the telephone?

Haven't you seen
The latest telegram?
Describing at length
My weight down to gram?

Is there an increase
Coming down the pike?
Provision with purpose
In a lighting strike?

Am I to receive
A bigger piece of slice?
Down to the penny
And at what price?

Has the time come
To simply recognize
My qualities, traits
Through the Father's eyes?

Am I to see
Who I really am?
Unblemished and clean
Gone all the blame?

With it the pain
And the suffering
Time for all gain
No more struggling?

Have I been freed
From the scales of past
Filled with His peace
That is meant to last?

Abundance and bliss
Have they now arrived?
Sweet morning kiss
Waking to sunrise.

Can I to love
As He loved me first?
Has the while come
For the outpour burst?

Tis' time to see
All His handy work?
Am I to fly free,
In gifts, new perk?

It must be so
As He said as much,
Revealing in glow,
His perfect touch.

14 Fullness of Time (Revival)

In fullness of time
The world is on fire,
Burn baby burn
Screaming revival.

Pour Jesus pour
Engulf in Your glory,
The rich and the poor
Finish Your story.

Mouths open wide
Bridge down the gap,
Heaven with earth collide
Rejoice and be glad.

Melt hardened hearts
Bitter hid re-reveal,
Connect all left-out parts
Of Your highlight reel.

Hit us with light
Of which we've never seen,
Unite us real tight
In one body and clean.

Are You really for sure,
Some call it for real,
Pure cloud of pure
Stepping down here?

Come Savior come
Without delay or pause,
Get to the root
Show us prime cause.

Show us for real
How selfish we've been,
How lost and confused
Just stuck in our sin.

Convict of all crime
Steeped deeply beneath,
Have every knee bow
With the fire You breathe.

The reckless self-will
Run riot in riots,
Chasing cheap thrill
Time for peace and quiet.

Time for a release
Of self-control and reigns,
Submit to Perfect Will
In revival of rain.

The end of time's here
In brand new terrain,
With Scriptures fulfilled
Revealing Your reign.

15 Tower's Fall (Repentance)

I'll raise you up from dead
With resurrect power,
Listen to what I'd said
Without trying harder.

Yield hardened heart of yours
From ivory tower,
My voice shall pour through pores,
For never prouder.

Yield more sweet child of mine
From defiance summit,
Leave high horses behind
By willing submit.

Come to Me come my love
All those heavy laden,
I offer lasting peace and rest
A safer haven.

I offer a transformed life
Translated over,
I supply all your needs
Over and over.

My will is absolute
Uncompromising,
The King's hand and resolute,
Shadowless shining.

Come down from Babylon,
Puffed up and prideful,
Get off the balloon you're on,
Disguising, spiteful.

Receive My words beloved
Swallowing sentence,
I am the One from above,
God of dependence.

It's Me you're relying on,
For each breath while taking,
For My glory and My awe,
Truly breathtaking.

If you would only know
Life's start and finish,
My awesome power, glow,
From start to finish.

The Alpha Omega Lord
The author of all,
Down to each dying breath
To end of your road.

The road that leads to Me
Through permit entrance,
Let go of self for Me,
Salvation repentance.

16 Love (Garden of Eden)

In warm summer embrace
touched by God's grace,
at last, love arrives
makes majestic entrance.

Inner sparks are now lit,
igniting hot fire,
souls separated by time
are quenched with desire.

Hearts beating real fast
and butterflies flying,
Phoenix's ashes ablaze,
it tickles, I'm crying.

Arms opened real wide
allowing for freedom,
with you naked I stand
back in the garden of Eden.

Your flower blooming anew
straight down overflow river,
born again not from womb
but by love's spirit quiver.

Savoring each every bite
as you reveal hidden treasure,
beauty's shine beyond sight
anticipating with pleasure.

As if waiting lifetimes
to return to your presence,
feel the heat, hear its rhyme,
to be back in the heavens.

To rediscover its sounds
every crevasse and alley,
to taste its nectar unbound
run down fruit orchard valley.

Back to the glory of God
our innocence restored,
let me now enter my love
together as one rejoined.

17 First Kiss (Reunited)

Dreaming of our first kiss
The taste of your lips,
Like honeycomb dew,
Sweet caramel drips.

Joined at the hips
Drink slowly, in sips,
True love express,
Crossing abyss.

Weak at the knees
Swarming of bees,
Shaking with shivers
Forevermore, please.

Flow state release
Freefall, at ease,
Hearts reunited,
Becoming one piece.

Steaming hot bliss
Melting moist mist,
The earth catching fire
Burning eclipse.

Nothing amiss
God's masterpiece,
Symmetry perfected
Stillness at peace.

Time standing still
Oneness fulfills,
Merging of mirrors
Infinite one kiss.

18 Muse Chasing

Chasing a muse in a maze
Dazed and confused,
Butterfly empty nets amaze
Am I saddened or amused?

Grasping to catch shorted breath
Clinching still air in hand,
Attempts filled with regret
Through fingers pouring of sand.

Porous pouring raindrops
Bedrock on a bed of rocks,
Gloomy sight of Christ's burning cross
When will our hearts come across?

Wide-gapped distance at hand
Melting icecaps afar,
Releasing signal through gland
Glance's shadow, how far?

Swamped in moistures of swamp
Neck down breath heavy still,
Waiting for signal, sign or a prompt,
For sudden opening to fill.

Windy blowing of ways
Which direction to take,
Room of mirrors ablaze
Are arrows pointing real, fake?

Flaky flakes of snowflake intent
Are her intentions for real?
Is dream reality bent,
Time warped, nothing to feel?

Her heart callused with pain
Hiding far behind fear,
Mind protected and trained
Keeping me stuck, sitting on pier.

Keeping me stuck far in a storm
Held under lock and at bay,
Her soul locked away, far from
Behind a wall of rocks and in clay.

Flood the earth again dear God,
Open hearts, heavens anew,
Send spirit, fire and love,
Revealing the Way we once knew.

19 Worlds Collide

On faith in action
is love here or missing?
Rolled-eyed reaction
And without kissing!

Of oil alabaster
Pouring anointing,
Spell grace or disaster?
Leaving me wanting.

More of You Father,
No fornicating,
For here, now, thereafter,
Marriage in making?

The Neeza commotion
Thru air arrow speeding,
Laughter in motion,
In no way receding.

Fired promotion
Don't leave me guessing,
Sarcastic love potion
Rudely progressing.

Wilder wildfire
Strong-willed crazed filly,
Her brimming desire
Not so seemingly silly.

Truthful reel reeling
See through undressing,
Two hearts' revealing
With each layer I'm pressing.

Peeling and peeling
Down to onion blooming,
Firestone corner,
Turnkey turn looming.

The air is polluting
And atmosphere building,
Inward revival,
More than gold-plated gilding.

God's hand assuming
Chiseling, grinding,
His time for pruning
For limits unbinding.

For real and not phony
For free and so freeing,
Is whole matrimony,
His gift of healing?

Two worlds colliding
To form edified being,
Through restless abiding
To love's own well-being.

20 Laying It Down (Thy Will Be Done)

How to be God's son
Of the One, Most High,
Is it a gift
Or do I have to try?

What is sonship
To be set afree,
Inheritance ship
Belonging to me?

To be knighted at night
Nicodemus' style,
Not by power's might
But in surrender's smile?

Or is it at cry,
When we lay all down.
Where, when and why,
Is mercy renowned?

Lay down my will
That which kept me stuck,
Remove it until
The tick's out, pluck.

Destiny's child
Or was it by dumb luck?
Was it at fate,
That the deal was struck?

How to get out
And turn my luck,
To receive instead
From the backed-up truck?

Saving from self
Is what's at stake,
Asking for help
Poor me forsake.

Stubbornness theft
The prideful foe,
The intruder has left
With his ego.

Go far now go,
You killer thief,
To too long ago,
Turning a new leaf.

Flee far away,
Away from here,
In dragon's slay,
I'm finally free.

Victory lap,
Of me I am none,
Two become one,
Thy Will be done.

21 Revealed (Thy Kingdom Come)

Who then is Jesus,
Immanuel?
Is He God with us,
Tell me, please, tell.

Tell telling signs
Is He Savior of all?
Forgiver of crimes,
Ever since fall?

Is He Lamb slain
Price sacrifice,
With nothing to gain
Is He the Christ?

Have we been told
On our road to hell,
To bondages sold,
To drink from His well?

Long been for-told,
To woman at well,
Unblinding the fold,
That all will be well.

Ring empty hollow
All other words,
Tough truth to swallow
Until it hurts.

Until it breaks
Myself and me in two,
Empties regrets
And my story too.

Until it reeks
Havoc unscrew,
Submerge valley peaks
Captain with crew.

Not 'til it fills
Fulfilling at last,
Mountains and hills,
Erasing the past.

Time standing still
At the awe of His sight,
It won't be until
All wrong is made right.

His time is here
For all stop and see,
For every ear hear
And all to be free.

The Father revealed
Through the work of His Son,
Every soul healed
Thy Kingdom come.

22 Filled (Born Again)

Overflow, grinning to the brim
Brimming with joy and a big grin,
Fill me, God, fill me past the brim
Heal every hole and branches trim.

Come Holy Spirit, come, dear friend,
Into each crevasse and loose end,
Erase me once more and anew,
Rewinding of old tapes, ways renew.

Rewinding of times stuck on repeat
Rid of me for good to last heart beat,
Finish the job so I am finished
Clean me O'Lord to unblemished.

Go on already and replenish
Restore me for good with Your finish,
Whatever it takes, all hands on deck
Wreck by encounter, please do wreck.

By all of your means of means to end
Crucify me, make my story end,
To the ends of the earth, past there too
Until I'm dead and the devil too.

Born me again, make me disappear
Clearly now clear blank slate appears,
Canvas of rope and Your helping hand
Pull me up steady in plan grand.

Out of my belly rivers now can flow
Levels of levies, water overflow,
Slowly then steadied pace supply
Mutter of tongues with music rhyme.

Angelic that voice and I hear it well
The Word of our Lord pouring out of well,
Springing to top after time in hell
Rising again through my every cell.

As I become one with the Son of man
Rendered beyond choice of who I am,
Living for Him with each dying breath
I'm born once more with no more death.

It's He that died for me so I could live
Lifting my burden and forgive,
Transacting of debt paid by sacrifice
With His very life as the only price.

He laid down for me so I could be free
Leaving me rested under shaded tree,
Doped up on hope instead of dope,
Swimming in love's sealed envelope.

Sealed by the mighty hand of God
Delivered, redeemed, and sanctified,
Finally set free by His mercy's grace
To overflow filled, in righteous place.

23 Yielded Vessel (Holy Grail)

A yielded vessel,
With anchor in place
Having fought, wrestled,
Overcame by grace.

Having endured
Life's stormy seas,
On land of bone dry
Seasons without peace.

Having been rebuilt
Even piece by peace,
Having fled rebellion,
From bondage released.

Having escaped
From the wilderness,
To having arrived
To its rightful place.

Submitted and laid
To the King of Kings,
No longer afraid
What weather brings.

Having surrendered
To His Perfect Love
To be used, rendered,
By His healing dove.

Having finally died
To the self itself,
After pleaded and cried,
Begged for help.

To His right standing
Having been re-led,
Through narrow gate landing
Nourished, fed.

Obedient submit
To pasture's graze,
To lighthouse summit
Fiery ablaze.

No longer a shipwreck
Outside of reach,
On this arduous trek,
Stuck on the beach.

From isolation
To His embrace,
From aimless wander
To Amazing Grace.

Finally at home
From broken, frail,
Restored in Surrender
By the Holy Grail.

24 Quarantined

I am dating a ghost
From an instagram post,
Elusive a muse
I am unable to host.

Crave more human touch
Am I asking too much?
These are quarantine rules
Era of end times and such.

Or of error of ways
Trapped by fear of always,
We've suddenly lost
Our meeting pathways.

Held at home and in traps
Waving through looking glass,
Isolation of old
Losing people and class.

Separation at hand
In an experiment grand,
Massive assault on mankind
Was it carefully planned?

Grimaces masked
Tasked with impossible task,
Separated by lines
Smiles revealing through cracks.

Or are they showing us frowns
With us dressed up as clowns,
Tragic comedy at play
In nuthouse exercise gowns.

Common good in disguise
Being touted surprise,
Give up freedom to see
A real human with eyes.

The lost seeking self help
Each on YouTube and Yelp,
Human touch disappear
In sea of seaweed and kelp.

Or did we all go astray
Chasing money and prey,
Obsessed with having more
Bling bling blindness of fame.

The blind leading the blind
Holding each other in bind,
Cattle call slaughterhouse
Terror of truth seems unkind.

Come now Savior now come
Of ourselves we're none,
Manifest heaven's gate
Let Thy Kingdom reign come.

25 Lightness of Being (Forgiveness Swim)

God's light in the darkness
Yoke's easy, lite harness,
Now let go of striving
For His energy harness.

Near sighted blindness
Was it covered by hardness?
Far off in the distance
My heart's beating heartless?

Speak to me Father
Speak louder and farther,
Release me the anointing
Your proud humbling prowess.

Release me from wanting
From bondages daunting,
Meet bitter with sweetness
Erase memories haunting.

Snow down flakes of glitter
From here to fore hither,
Slow down all past motions
Stop time, reconsider.

Court cases of healing
Mercy's touch revealing,
The lifting of all curses
In motions and appealing.

Emotions empty scoresheet
Render blame and treat,
Removing all the shrapnel
Precision scalpel, concrete.

Turn from spotty spotless
Dress up topless, countless,
Wreck me by encounter
Whore made virgin countess.

Throw out the main critic
And bags that come with it,
Touch me with your fire,
Come now, Holy Spirit.

So patient with each patient
No rationing adjacent,
It's intentional drowning
In forgiveness sea station.

Is this to know Jesus
The who, the way that He is?
Sufficient in His grace
In all that which pleases.

The light weight of His glory
Repentance, truly sorry,
Love's great redeeming,
For His sake and His story.

26 Broken Heart (A Cry for Help)

Dear God heal broken heart
My Love, Mi Corazon,
Move shut door open real hard,
Chess pieces across chest repawn.

In pieces again and yet still
Crack me open real wide,
Refill this human landfill
Vastly erasing the divide.

Rid me of my selfish will
Reveal Your purposed one instead,
Hold me up steady and still
Feed me turned water with bread.

Win me over in a landslide
Slide over king, bishop, and rook,
Dismantle hidden arrogance, pride
Unhooking enemy's hook.

Swim me across this filth of flesh
Served up cup of sweat's pouring stench,
Memory of wholeness refresh
My lonesome loneliness quench.

Water seeds of truth and much more
Help me get out of myself,
Grow there Your garden galore
With blossom's blooms on each shelf.

Undress me from this tangled web
Of lies postering straight,
Release me from heaviness' lead
Hear me, I am crying for help!

Get me off hamster wheel grind
In circles where run into walls,
Offer new view, open mind,
The splendor of expanse's white halls.

Reshape ways, landscapes indeed
Redrawing borders of maps,
With perfect precision and speed
Open circuits of blindly closed laps.

Open eyelids widely held shut
Hardened strongholds do melt,
Discharge infected puss, leave cut
Heal every battered bruise felt.

Reimburse too what devil took
Reversing false charges in full,
Break what his hands knowingly shook,
All past agreements annul.

Grant me freedom to live
Experience joy, laughter, true love,
Let me be happy receiving, too give,
Knowing it's all from above.

27 Ease Release (Redemption)

Abundance a dance
Stilled-framed a glance,
Just a moment in time
Or prolonged a stance?

Glimmer of lasting peace
A small piece of release,
Or a restoration in full,
And an end of disease?

Am I finally at ease
After sorries with pleas,
And a few broken hearts,
Bruised begging scraped knees?

Say it is so, say please,
Sunshine's summer sea breeze,
Having passed the dark skies
For love's healing degrees.

Do I now get to live
Fully breathe and forgive,
Experience a pure joy
Freely receive and to give?

Do I know how to stand
On my two feet in sand,
Have I been humbled to see
To comprehend, understand?

Do I get what life is
Creation and bliss,
Do I now feel with my heart,
Taste the taste of each kiss?

Gone the gone missing miss
No to regret, reminisce,
It all shaped me to be
A great man and His.

Having stared down abyss
Broken, empty, dismissed,
Having risen from ash
I get to share all of this.

That the One above's true
Faithful, holy and pure,
Epistle's pen's redeemed
Prescription writing cure.

That the healing will last
Grace erasing the past,
Freedom has now arrived
Putting first those were last.

Glory be to our God
Head up held high in nod,
Rallying lion's roar
In hand buckler with rod.

28 Night Call (Awakenings)

Should I pray or masturbate
The night's own daily dilemma,
Fallen's deeper has my state
Saint with salmonella?

Human nature then you say
Diseased row of champions,
Disappear or shall I stay
To realize His grand visions?

In black and whitely paradox
Messy hair of precision,
Perfectly built body ox
Wrapped in indecision.

By dying I'm to come alive
How difficult to reconcile,
In letting go I stop to strive
Genius that's gone senile.

Is the world turned upside down
Here or in Kingdom to come,
Is servant King with thorny crown
Are we called to become one?

Wake me up to fall asleep
Is this the great awakening?
In my heart or down the street
Is revival happening?

Am I here to love them all
The crazies and the lunatics,
Am I one too after all
With my big mouth politics?

Stilly loud, seems indiscreet
The Lord's voice inside my head,
Verses ringing on repeat
Turn I back to bed instead?

Or do I rise to answer call
Steadied steadfast obedience,
Do I live to give it all
As He did through innocence?

Do I share and make sacrifice
My time, talent, bounty small,
Am I prepared too to pay a price
To stand firm, strong and tall?

Impatient in long-suffering
The hour struck true honesty,
To persevere through struggling
To grow wings of His majesty.

In surrender to His perfect love
Jesus, please take all of me,
Father, Son, and the Holy Dove
Through faith truth let my eye see.

29 Air

Of Air and not Aires
That so evenly varies,
Breathe her in deeply,
With all that she carries.

Strong and vivacious
Often randomly gracious,
Awkward in her charm,
Spirit's roomy and spacious.

She's part Gemini beauty
Soft cuddling cutie,
With pieces of Pisces,
Bright smile, bit moody.

Seemingly off balance
Reaction of valence
Sweetly delicious,
Ambitiously freelance.

Longing to free dance
Flow posturing romance,
Glow's healing a sparkle
Here by fate or by chance?

Illuminating that vision
Of souls' head collision
Her glances so piercing,
Reveal hearts' position.

It's the bite of the apple
With which I must grapple,
Taste buds awaken,
To the filly in saddle.

Move sideways and straddle
Or to heart of the battle
The walls' crumbling down,
Fear's cages sound rattle.

Straight to core of her essence
To sit in that presence,
Screams loud for allowing
In present and past tense.

Where are you taking me
Are we to be free?
To enter love's free fall
For once, for all to see?

Is that the end there in sight,
Would you grant me the insight?
Is God's hand working here,
To walk by faith and not sight?

So go on, keep guessing
With heat's rise progressing,
Petaled layers falling
Discover steeped blessing.

30 The Unlovable's Love (Repentance Void)

How to love the unlovable
What a lovely lullaby,
The spotty and questionable,
The guilty without alibi.

How to touch the untouchable
Teach me, I'm out of touch,
The untouched, unapproachable,
Ones' hit with life's sucker punch.

How to reach the unreachable,
All that seems so out of reach,
How to teach the unteachable
The lonely souls and spirits each.

Just how do we minister
To the ones just beyond reach?
To the once proud and sinister,
Teach me, please do me teach.

And how to preach the desirable
To the lost, undesirable,
How to bring them the good news,
To vie back the unviable?

How to stitch back the broken piece
Of the snitch and the burglar too,
To bring in piece of lasting peace
To the one who's cut in two?

To the hangman and the cutter too,
How to show them they are loved?
The kidnapped daughter on rendezvous
With evil's face through raping shove.

The war-torn hero, the veteran,
The one hearing voices, what to do then?
What about me, she won't look at me,
Unwilling to come near glaring STD?

The fall-down drunk and the addict such,
Could it be so they've been through too much?
With too many wounded scars to close,
With too many no's to oppose?

Do they just collect what the reaper sowed,
In their neglect or life's broken bow,
Do they receive a true second chance,
Will they enjoy their wedding's first dance?

Can King Jesus truly heal us all
I hear about it, but I would like to know,
I read about it, but I would like to see
With my own two eyes, and be set free.

Came to us Father, please show Your face,
I've made a mess here, in disgrace,
In Godly sorrow, in repentance void,
Come to us Abba, please don't avoid.

31 Grace

What then is Grace?
An emptying space
Of infinite wisdom,
Touch without trace?

New door in place
A portal in space,
Transporting movement
A gift wrapped in lace?

A run past the race
With all past erase,
He said it's finished
In tightly embrace.

An unearned favor
A brand new flavor,
A fresh beginning
Right now and later.

Maybe forever
When we're together,
In free fall and falling
Lighter than feather.

Slowly now breathing
Peaceful receiving
Two become oneness,
Heartbeats stop beating.

Profoundly pleasing
Burdens releasing,
Unyoked of bondage
Stillness appeasing.

Callused to smooth top
With each every oil's drop,
Anointing of heavens
Flowing and won't stop.

Revival pour down
From head, toe, and crown
Floodgates of glory,
On every house in town.

Look who's calling
The sick and appalling,
Unparalleled gifting
To those and the crawling.

What of the upright
The self-righteous and uptight,
They, too, receive mercy
Undarkened by the light?

The healing is lasting
To all without casting,
To every last soulmate
Beyond everlasting.

32 Alive (Words)

Painstakingly staking
With each step that I'm taking,
The clock keeps on ticking
In this grand undertaking.

Still restless in resting
Being tested through testing,
The arrows keep pointing
The eggs hatch while nesting.

No more of hiding
It's time for abiding,
The moment of releasing
With resistance subsiding.

From glory to glory,
Such a triumphant story,
Written all down while pacing
On kitchen's wood story.

The back and forth moving
With eyesight improving,
Pour into me, Father,
That still voice approving.

While need to prove nothing
You chose whom that was nothing,
Only broken and battered
As to showcase Your real thing.

The deep waters now gushing
Life's energy rushing,
The rebirth of dead man
From under blows crushing.

Bring on revival
Down to meek street arrival,
Let them feel presence
Found on pages of Bible.

For those faithfully walking
And the painfully balking,
Faithfulness to unfaithful
And those seeking and stalking.

Pour out Your mercy
On the foul mouths still cursing,
On the ones too singing praises
In voice choir rehearsing.

Speak life and words nursing
Ways, directions reversing,
Let all stand alive in You
In love's perfect immersing.

Without delay and more swiftly
Come now, before I'm fifty,
Or whenever You want to
For the messy, too, nifty.

33 The Turn (New Leaf)

Sun-kissed at dawn
Well beyond yawn,
Beyond all the fray
Mundane and gray.

Promised at noon
The stars and the moon,
Sweetness caress
My chest tighly press.

Fogging the breath
Rebirth from death,
Catharsis of soul
Unshattered and whole.

With you alone
Released from the prone,
Straight jacket's gone
Free to go on.

Free to go roam
The pedestrian zone,
Liberated to look
Under each unturned stone.

Kiss now each frog
Through mirage of fog,
Through clutter distract
For the one piece in tact.

Turn over new leaf
Relieving relief,
Discovering gold
Buried under my grief.

Hidden way down below
The dark smothering glow,
Heat's rising above
Melt ice capping flow.

Revealing bright shine
Two heartbeats combine,
Pulled forward by force
That's charting my course.

Drawn straight to the light
To the eye of eyesight,
To the eye of the storm
To that above norm.

Off to unusual love
Through mountains of tough,
Through the steepest of climbs
Down poetic verse rhymes.

It's ascending descent
Graceful beyond decent,
The loverboy's free-fall
To the deep that knows end.

34 New Season

Peaceful forrest sleeps
Menories lost keeps,
The keeper of our words
Thruthful truth it breaths.

In it offspring breeds
In spring fresh blood bleeds,
With it new life brings
In which scar disappears.

From shadow light appears
For drag queens and the queers,
The straight ones too alike
New hope reappears.

In front and arrears
Head from ground it rears,
Mushroom cloud meadow
Wiping off old tears.

Welcome in the sun
Shining all and some,
Radiate each soul,
Of Father and the Son.

Flood all free indeed
The broken ones in need,
Those who've traveled far
Off course breaking speed.

Breaking bones in two
By choice or those forced to,
Loosing way alone,
In bathrooms, in bars too.

The sitting behind bars
The others crashing cars,
With them shatter dreams
In burnt out house of cards.

On course taking lead
Fully now proceed,
Liberate us good,
To win and to succeed.

Catch the beastly beast
Cleanse mold's rising yeast,
Insidious old foe
Ruining kingly feast.

Royal that mistake
For the bait to take,
To think that it could win
And His throne overtake.

With stillness and with peace
Manifest release,
Penetrate our hearts
Slowly piece by piece.

35 In Hearts

In hearts of mine and men
Reveal Yourself dear God,
In hearts of mine and then
Speak Word's fullness and out loud.

In hearts of mine and when
I meet You face to face at last,
In hearts of mine and them
Unshackle hostages of past.

In hearts of mine and us
Unite heavens with the earth,
In hearts of mine and plus
Its width with length across the girth.

In hearts of mine and yours
All alone traveling this world,
In hearts of mine and those
Unblinding vision's eyesight blurred.

In hearts of mine and all
The fallen too, the, proud,
In hearts of mine and tall
The short, quiet, and much too loud.

In hearts of mine and such
Of diseased character defect,
The mental rentals not worth much
Those geniuses too, to perfect.

In hearts of mine and now
Come Holy Spirit, please just come,
In hearts of mine and how
Turnaround sound of heartbeat drum.

In hearts of mine and still
Hold steady shaking hands and feet,
In hearts of mine and fill,
The missing piece of empty street.

In hearts of mine and too
Minds, spirits and dry bones,
In hearts of mine and into,
The cored rocky wall of stones.

In hearts of mine one, two,
Pour out Your healing glory through,
In hearts of mine and to,
Heart of the matter through and thru.

In hearts of mine and ours
The loved ones up close and afar,
In hearts of mine and scars,
Of broken pieces shattered jar.

In hearts of mine and theirs
The ones that hurt us, some real bad,
In hearts of mine and stares,
All damaged ones to be made glad.

In hearts of mine, where else
You are making new abode,
In hearts of mine and cells
You are imprinting there Your code.

In hearts of mine and more
You are restoring all galore,
In hearts of mine, in store,
You are repairing each cold sore.

In hearts of mine and there
You are lifting me up for good,
In hearts of mine and care,
You are telling me I could.

In hearts of mine and this
You are showing me I can,
In hearts of mine abyss,
You are turning me into a man.

In hearts of mine down deep
You are teaching me to give,
In hearts of mine up steep
You are allowing me forgive.

In hearts of mine last time
You are showing me Your heart,
In hearts of mine each rhyme,
You are making a fresh start.

In hearts of mine and men
The unveiling of your love,
In hearts of mine, again
Lies freedom's Holy dove.

In hearts mine, each breath,
Lies life's reason to go on,
In hearts of mine, in death,
'Til final exhale's passing on.

36 Violin (Heart Yearning)

Her eyes a violin
Sound to my very heart,
With no stings attached
When will recital start?

Her eyes a violin
Pure music to my ears,
Note-noted state I'm in,
Which all noise disappears.

It's all I hear is love,
Her heartbeat violin,
It's all I feel and be enough
Arrive to place I've never been.

How dear her violin,
With each tone neatly toned
To die in her, to every sin,
To die in love, ravished and stoned.

Her eyes a violin
With all past well-postponed
Is now my fall for her begin,
In which a new life formed?

Her eyes a violin
A window to my soul,
Her every glance to underpin
Sightseeing healed of every hole.

Her eyes a violin
It's now I enter love?
Exiting all I've ever been,
Erasing scars of sea-waves rough.

Her eyes a violin
Pull pull on gentle strings,
An angel's movement through my skin
Embrace of heaven brings.

Her eyes a violin
With every triad gently played,
Allowing me to go on in,
Dragons of haunt defeated, slayed.

Her eyes a violin
How sweet this melody,
To drown in her well past my chin
Floating on air spa remedy.

Her eyes a violin
Down to last every chord,
Conquering prince atop in win
Raising heart vibration sword.

Her eyes a violin
In which I've overcome,
Defeated doubt that hid within,
Yearning for earning her heart's sum.

37 Kingdom Love

The one that uplifts
From downward down-drifts,
From doubtful seasons,
Defying reasons.

Defying our best thought
Spoken of or taught,
Deafening white noise
Calming of distraught.

Calming of rough seas
Until the blind sees,
Until the dead rise,
Pleasing to disease.

It's one that speaks life
Makes peace in all strife,
Such love that covers
Your back and frostbite.

Of wisdom, foresight,
Inside of insight,
The very heart of God,
Infinite bright light.

All-catching in weakness
Humble as meekness,
In moments of blunder
Enlightening thunder.

Softness of petal,
The gold of gold medal,
Inviting upwards,
Past voices that settle.

It's there to build up
Press through the build up,
Of defenses' fences,
Hurts and offenses.

The one that brings smiles
In desperate dark trials,
To tears through make up,
Turns cheeks and makes up.

It's there to love you
Nurture and ground you,
Down to soul level,
Bedevil the devil.

Is known as freedom
Reminds where you came from,
Allowing for mistake
For each one to remake.

Some call her reckless
Pearl of pearl necklace,
The hope of glory
Unblemished, speckless.

38 Falling in Love (One Hundred Percent)

One hundred percent for love
Or is it a hundred and ten?
Am I falling down to above
Am I falling for her, right there 'n' then?

From up close and from afar,
Blessed by her in every way,
As if heaven's bright chosen star,
Has down descended to play.

As if answer arrived overnight
To endless prayers at night,
As if enlightened by a new light
That feels custom-fitted and right.

Am I head over heels, too, overhead,
Is this to happen for real?
With every step now being led,
Is this how love's feelings do feel?

Do I know what's lying ahead,
Will I be gifted her heart?
Pure love, pulse bloody and red,
Wipe away tears in a new start.

Am I upside down spinning in reels
In her beauty of radiant rays,
Is this the sunlight that heals,
The awaited arrival that stays?

Is this reversal of luck
To unfold atop folded hand,
In moving pass go, the unstuck,
Do I at love's door finally stand?

Or a magic touch of His grace
Of divine encounter with greet,
Is this falling in love and in place,
From the very first time of our meet?

Is this alignment indeed
Of mountains moving across,
Is this the time of God's speed
Of glorious restore of loss?

Is this the evidence longly hoped for
Of the things seeming unseen,
The manifest opening door
To a life with her as queen?

Am I truly that truly blessed,
To have found her in moment of chance?
Am I to know, not only guess,
With each passing day of her glance?

Will I to live what love is
Through her in united bond,
Will I receive such mercy of His,
Free to let go and love her beyond?

39 Healed

What does it mean,
to be healed?
Whole and complete,
Sanctified, sealed?

Blameless and clean,
Whole, on a roll,
Is it self-acceptance
A purified soul?

Is it soundness of mind,
In rhythm and rhyme?
To no longer collide
With the One from above?

Is it sweetness of tongue,
A turned rosy cheek,
An awakened spirit,
Clarity of speech?

Or is it contentment,
Nothing to crave,
Feeling each breath,
And riding the wave?

With no strife nor to strive,
Nowhere to reach,
Push, pull or hide,
To take all in stride?

Is it to make love,
On a slow afternoon,
To the love of your life,
And again the next noon?

Or is it to give,
Of yourself and more,
To selflessly serve,
Not longing for more?

Or is it to know
Who am I and why,
Having been created
With purpose in mind?

Is it allowing,
Moving downstream
With arms wide open,
Embracing this dream?

Or a walk in the woods,
In deep ocean's swim,
Is it bathing in grace
Atop rainbow's rim?

Maybe it's compassion,
The capacity to feel,
The other's joy, pain,
A sign of being healed?

Or is it a release,
A complete letting go,
In sweet surrender,
And trusting the flow?

Is it a song
A dance in the rain?
Shedding all pain,
Be no longer insane?

Is it hugging real tight
Just like you mean it?
All wrongs be made right
Would you believe it?

Or is it a state,
of being, clean slate,
A posture long held,
With promises kept?

Is it each cell,
Well-balanced and fed?
Is it disciplined freedom
God's Word digested and read?

Or is it forgiveness,
An emptying heart,
Free of hard rocks
Weighing it down?

Perhaps it's to live,
and not to be dead,
abundantly full,
With every need met?

Or a glimmer of hope,
Joy found in Christ,
Climb mustard seed rope,
Beyond reason or price?

Is it moving through fear
To whole another gear,
Is it death to the self
And asking for help?

Is it everyday life
Done with a smile,
With innocence felt
Of freed inner child?

I think that is it,
God's love and pure joy,
Ignited and lit,
As the healing for all.

It is His love,
Seed sown long ago,
In hearts having sprouted
And beautifully grown.

40 Forty

Forty years,
in the wilderness,
Forty years,
and no less.

Forty years,
of loneliness,
The time has come,
take deep breaths.

The time is here,
to reappear,
It is now,
to reconcile.

To be still
and know I am God,
And have been,
all the while.

The time is here,
With end near,
His voice's heard
Loud and clear.

Forty years
in the past,
Freedom march
and at last.

Forty poems
through the roams,
The time has come,
work is done.

The time is here
to draw near,
To rest in Me
and be free.

To abide
in the vine,
Forty years
csossing line.

Come across
to the Cross,
Come across,
the finish line.

To finished work,
It is done,
Come across,
through the One.

Come over
Cross boarder,
Past the sand,
To promise land.

Milk, honey
Springing well,
Life water,
All is well.

Soaring wings
Happenings,
Saving grace
Righteous place.

Forty years,
Past stubbornness,
Mercy's touch
Of Holiness.

Forty years
Cleansing tears,
Forgiven now,
Breathe and bow.

Father's heart,
Gift revealed,
In book of life
Pages sealed.

www.ingramcontent.com/pod-product-compliance
Lightning Source LLC
Chambersburg PA
CBHW070949180426
43194CB00041B/1992